Roath Writers

2023 Anthology

Copyright © 2023 Roath Writers

All rights reserved. This book or any portion thereof may not be reproduced or used in any manner whatsoever without the express written permission of the publisher except for the use of brief quotations in a book review or scholarly journal.

First Edition: 2023

ISBN: 9798862259759

With heartfelt thanks to the Roath Writers interns who made this anthology happen: Pete Gaskell and Rhiannon Griffiths.

Thanks to Simon Read
for the brilliant cover design.

Thank you to the Mackintosh Sports Club and Community Centre for giving us a wonderful new home.

For more information about other exciting groups or events happening at the Mackintosh please visit their website:

http://mackintoshsportsclub.org/

Contents

Introduction: Christina Thatcher   1

Another Night at Roath Writers 6th June 2023:
Francess   3

The Street Cats of Lockdown: Osian Luke   5

Euphoria: Baz Greenland   7

Deal: Bryan Marshall   9

Date #1: Simon Read   10

H2O: William Dean Ford   12

**Watch the water from the mountain trickle where it
wants, :** Dervla O'Brien   13

Fallowing: Mat Troy   14

Highlights and Freedom: Rufus Mufasa   16

Pony (Photo): Stephen Andrews   18

The Willow Tree: Baz Greenland   19

The Book of Love: Andrew Davies   21

The Seventh Time They Fucked For The Last Time (Or The Slow Painful Death of a Toxic Affair):
William Dean Ford 23

Fingers and Toes: Baz Greenland 25

Blood and balls.: Andy Caruana 28

Bad Sport: Bryan Marshall 29

Joe: Rachel Badger 30

& then you came along: Dervla O'Brien 31

Gnawing: Alexander Winter 33

When I Say Rhythm: Gordon Anderson 34

3 minutes.: Andy Caruana 35

Fluid. Singular.: Simon Read 36

Care: Bryan Marshall 38

Reclining Chair: Osian Luke 39

Adrenochrome: Francess 41

The Angel Hotel: Rachel Badger 42

The Recording Angel: Barbara Hughes-Moore	44
A Lovely Verse: Alexander Winters	48
Crown of Creation: Pete Gaskell	49
Salvation: Francess	51
sound of a break: Dervla O'Brien	53
Mother of the Sad Clowns: Osian Luke	55
Letter to my Family: Dee Dickens	57
Our Mother Tongue: Rachel Badger	59
The Internal Friction of Those Required To Bow: William Dean Ford	60
For They/Them: Rufus Mufasa	61
Pony and Birds (Photo): Stephen Andrews	63
Biographies	65

Introduction

Some might say that 11 years isn't a special anniversary. After all, it's not one of those 'milestone' numbers – not a 5 or a 10 or a 15 or a 20. It is an in-between year. But this week, I learned that, in numerology, 11 is a 'Master Number' with all kinds of connections to rebellion, extravagance, conflict, remembrance, knowledge, duality and creativity. And so much of this is what we are celebrating here!

In this anthology, you will see many things: cards, cats, chairs, ponies, trees, angels, love. You will see relationships unfolding, excellent dialogue and very funny jokes. And beneath it all is the hum of our community – every laugh, every hug, every clink of our pint glasses.

This year our members settled into our hybrid rhythm: attending both online meetings and in person ones at The Mackintosh. Some shared drafts in our Facebook group while others sent texts or wrote emails about their progress. This anthology acts as a celebration of the varied and dynamic work we have produced over this year. Each piece was inspired by a Roath Writers' session.

This anthology also acts as a reflection of the last 11 years we have spent together. Together, I hope these pieces act as a small testament to our big community. I can't wait to see what the next year brings!

Christina Thatcher
Founder and Facilitator of Roath Writers
@RoathWriters

Quote submitted by Dee Dickens

'I'm only here to find out what happened to Uncle Einon's glass eye.'

— Dylan Thomas, probably.

Another Night at Roath Writers 6th June 2023

Not in the converted church now called The Gate,
but in The Mackintosh Sports and Racquet Club,
Roath where we previously read poems
some years ago at Rhyme and Real Ale

A life time ago: pre COVID
when I shook like a jelly fish on a vibroplate
when reading my words, many of us shook
and now, our world has been shaken.

I still look out on the bowling green
I like green, I need to see green, green spaces
I love green grass, plants, trees and clean sky.

I know there is a community garden behind there, somewhere.
Some poet's sport was, is rolling rollies.
Tonight, I can see the non grass, yet green tennis courts
laden with balls, racquets and most likely, non writers.

We read and study a poem;
'Another Night in Bourbon Street' by Christie Collins
I wonder, Bourbon the drink or Bourbon the city?
Perhaps both.

Our theme is to write on 'Another Night in… '
I choose Roath Writers, The Mackintosh,
I haven't been for a long time as I don't like online,
Does that make me 'old fashioned' or just real?

I observe writers at the table, I see thoughts being penned, pens moving,
writers thinking, using the thinking pose: the ESR pose; hands on
foreheads, looking up, wondering, remembering, imagining,
creating words on a theme, on their chosen theme, or dream.

The miracle is like us: no two pieces are ever the same.

Francess

The Street Cats of Lockdown

I walk these sullen, statuesque streets.
Rare passersby are concealed by mask or snood.
It's the apocalypse no one saw coming.
A boring one.

Twice a day I keep these atrophied limbs moving
Twice a day I take a circuitous route to nowhere
To sanity? To survival? maybe?

Down a half-beaten track I amble
And it's there that I encounter you-
A gang of fluffy delinquents
Tail deep in a bin.

For you little munchkins
The world is now your meatstick.
With your silent padding paws and
Slender, hungry maws
You now see a world hollowed of dangers.

Cars run seldom and
bipedal threats have largely retreated
Though I'm sure the dropped rubbish has declined-
Those brimming burrows of leftover crumbs.

Sometimes, though, the feast follows the famine.
You hear a rumour from some felines down Gabalfa
That the binmen have migrated
Leaving their precious cargo unguarded.

You collude with the seagulls,

Those blackhearted knaves,
To tip and tear and rip and break open
Just about whatever you can.

And into the space where danger once lurked,
There is now opportunity.

Emboldened are the little birds,
And in their foolish confidence
They flutter, carefree, in your focused path.
Like wetfood falling into a bowl.

No wonder you are so stunned then
As I happen across you
Beside this half-wooded creek
Raiding an upturned bin.

Your pupils stretch wide, wider than width,
And in my lockdown delirium
I hear you blurt out, I think:
"I thought you bipedal pricks were extinct!"

Osian Luke

Euphoria

I wait. Waiting. Waiting for…
To pick me up.
To swing me in the air.
To tickle me.
To laugh.
I wait. Waiting. Waiting for…
And the waiting never stops.

My kids don't have to wait.
I pick them up.
I swing them in the air.
Their giggling with slightly panicked fright,
as I throw them higher and higher,
limbs flailing, belly laughs rippling,
wide-eyed manic euphoria

I'm still waiting.
There's anticipation as I swing gently back and forth.
He's in the park with us. Is this the first time?
And I want him to push,
push me higher and higher,
until I cling with desperation against the metal chains as my legs kick the air!
But he's not here. He's on the bench and he's looking anywhere but at me,
And I kick back and swing, but the euphoria never comes.

My kids don't have to wait.
I pull them back until my arms ache.
They giggle with anticipation as they ascend into the air.
Kick those legs! Watch them fly!

Wind sweeping back their fluffy hair,
Cold wind stinging their eyes and they don't care.
One and then the other, I'm like a well-oiled machine,
pushing them higher and higher.
And they don't want to stop.
More! More! More!

Mum knows how to tickle.
How to get me under the ribs and that sweet spot,
until I giggle and I laugh and my stomach aches.
But he's just sitting there,
looking anywhere other than me.
Mum's a tickle monster,
Dad's just a...

I'm the world's greatest tickle monster,
flickering fingers on tummies and knees.
Giggles and belly laughs,
a relentless onslaught of fun.
Too much fun?
Maybe I'm trying too hard?
But I'd rather they have too much than wait.
Wait. Waiting. Waiting for...
The euphoria that never comes.

Baz Greenland

Deal

Of all the skies to fall under,
you chose the one clouded by me.

Slight blue,
light wind,
a breath just
caught.

Then, too late, burdened, tormented,
you dealt me again
another strange hand.

New, stranger, bolder stars.

A glance, something shining, fixed in
a c o n s t e l l a t i o n

Your move, and the heavens
press themselves into our eclipse.

Bryan Marshall

Date #1

We sat across from one another temporarily, until I remembered what this was and re-positioned myself so if she was twelve o'clock, I was nine.

"Drinks?" a waiter asks, causing us to mumble to each other and ourselves while fumbling through the menu. This action is performative, and we order our respective defaults.

"Excellent," the waiter says with a smile; again, performative. "I'll bring them over shortly!"

A few drinks. She's laughing at almost nothing and sometimes actually nothing. Our fingers interlace between her spontaneous firework-like hand expressions before the dalliance of digits resumes.

Dessert arrives. She grabs a spoon with a "squeeee!" only a true sweet treat enthusiast would make.

"Ita-daki-mas!" She's Japanese. Actual Japanese, as opposed to some westerner with a cultural fetish. She's from Tokyo, which I understand makes this story less interesting, but the story is true and it's where she's from. I didn't know what itadakimas meant at the time, but I do now.

"Hmmm!" she grabs my wrist. Her eyebrows jump ropes. She has since switched to a new drink, having had enough time to peruse the menu. A gimlet. She slams the empty glass down.

"Ya know," she says. "There… should be an evil Halloween version of Santa."

"Yeah?" is all I can say after gulping down my eighth default drink.

"On a sleigh pulled by moths!"

"And… and you leave a plate of bellybutton lint out on Halloween Eve."

"With a… a… mug of Ovaltine!" she adds. I don't get it.

"And… err… Halloween carols sung by choirs of concussed children!" I add.

She looks away, as if trying to find somebody.

We say not another word. Our fingers interlock in a new configuration.

The waiter returns.

Simon Read

H2O

You're my H2O (Dew upon the petals of the sweet pink rose)

Rain storm (Soak a tree to the roots)

The quivering puddle (For my wellington boots)

You're my cup of tea (Delicate jasmine scent for me)

You're my morning mist (Getting lost in you then off you drift)

You're my mountain spring (brook, stream, then river when you're flowing)

You're my shoreline foam (when the wave that crashes carries me home)

You're my thunder cloud (Majestic in the air over cowering ground)

Satiating the thirst of beasts

Holy Water for non-pious priests

Liquid sin wash away my woes

You're my H2O

William Dean Ford

Watch the water from the mountain trickle where it wants,

down the lanes, down the rocks.
In the marshy rivershade, life experiments with
sculpture. It forms a chemical system of response

To the cold and dappled December light.
The frost writes a mathematical paper on
fractal shapes. The mycelial networks
invent their own electrical grid.

The mountain water pushes into town
finds itself held in the outer bailey of a fortress canal.
Moss climbs the concrete cracks, pushed back by
scores of herbicides on each side.

In the city, pools of water bubble dark,
reflecting slick with sickly oil.

Dervla O'Brien

Fallowing

(Inspired by the Tafod y Llew/Bristly Oxtongue painting, part of Braenaru/Fallowing exhibition by Seren Stacey at Dinefwr)

I, in your words,
Open my eyes again.
This time in a place
I have not known
Since before
cement and stone
Laid down lines,
And blade and spade
Forbade me
This space.
This year,
You left the earth
Fallow.
My seeds
In the atmosphere
Found landing,
And once bird,
Baking sun,
And bare feet,
Had taxed the scatterlings,
I took root.
I would whisper
My thanks,
If my voice
Were anything more
Than the caress of the wind
On my fractal form.

Whether my touch
And movement
Is oxen or lion to you,
Is not important.
This is
A silent moment,
Between you and I
As we enjoy
Our moment in the sun

Mat Troy

Highlights & Freedom

Merlyn gwyllt gyda naws y nawdegau
fel hysbysfwrdd ar gyfer *Sun In*
a teulu o Bondai a Nimbin.

Dirlawn gan dywalltiad o gusanau haul
yn rhoi i chi eich glow J Lo
i carnau'r ddaear gyda'ch Bronx.

Eich rhediadau Gwyddelig Llychlynnaidd
croes wrteithio gyda Kurt Cobain
Smells like Teen Spirit.

Where did you sleep last night?
dan y ser gyda Duw yn dyst,
calon yn canu mewn curiad
rhydd-id-rhydd-id-rhydd-id

Highlights & Freedom

Wild pony with 90's vibes
Looking like a billboard for *Sun In*
Your roots in Bondai & Nimbin.

Saturated by sun-kisses
That give you that J-Low glow
Hoofing the ground with your Bronx.

Your Viking Irish streaks
Crossfertilised with Kurt Cobain
Smells Like Teen Spirit.

Where did you sleep last night?
Under the stars with God as my witness
Heart singing to the beat of
rhydd-id rhydd-id rhydd-id

Rufus Mufasa

Pony – Stephen Andrews

with special thanks to People Speak Up

The Willow Tree

On Manor Road, with the willow tree,
sun rippling through the golden
branches hanging lazily in the summer sun,
and the grass, emerald green

But this abundance of life,
rich, infused with colour and sunshine.
A lazy summer afternoon in my childhood,
feels sepia and wan, and hazy, and lost

I understand the expectation of joy,
that burgeoning glut of childhood memories
should invite me in under that willow tree.
But it's all sepia, and grey, and dust

I fight to remember that childhood home,
that place where joy should have taken root.
And in its place, my memories broken,
a suffocating chasm of darkness

There's a yard all dust and brick,
and red tiles on the kitchen wall,
where ants burst in one summer afternoon,
and swarmed like black oil on my childhood home

It's darkness and ants.
And force-fed dinners.
There's a fleeting thought of pizza,
but all I can see are kidney beans, and ants, and tears

I try to remember that childhood home,

with the golden willow tree in the front garden.

But all I can see are pitch chasms where the rooms should be,
and the waiting for family and joy to begin

All I can see is the colour black,
and the waiting, and waiting, and waiting for life to begin.
And in that waiting, that grey depression,
that permeates the house on Manor Road

With the willow tree

Baz Greenland

The Book of Love

Based on The Book of Tobit

The fish entrails eked goop and grime onto Tobias's hands. Its flesh filled his belly as he sat in the dirt, ruminating on the Angel's words. It told him Sarah was beautiful, and that as her closest living relative, he had every right to take her as his wife. It told him that she cried out for God's help every night.

Tobias had told the Angel he knew of Sarah; that she was beautiful, and that she was cursed. He knew that a demon slept in her chambers, and murdered every husband she married on the night of her wedding. She had now taken seven husbands, and all of them had shuffled their mortal coil.

Tobias knew the whispers beneath the story: that some suspected Sarah herself. The Angel asked if he thought those whispers to be true. Tobias said no. He trusted his kin.

The Angel had asked if Tobias questioned the path set out for him by the Lord; Tobias shook his head. He was a man of God. He had the entrails. He would use them.

***

Sarah watched as Tobias lit the fire, an orange glow steadily filling the room. The incense sat unused in the corner. Instead, he tossed the entrails onto the flames. The newlyweds watched as the guts burned into a mushy brown paste.

They waited. Emptiness and silence met them.

"I don't understand," said Tobias, "The Angel said this would trap the demon, that it -"

"There was no demon. There was only me." A blaze of holy light saw the chamber fill with the Angel, flaming, wheeling, winged.

"I didn't want to marry," said Sarah, "so I called out to the Lord, asking for grace and mercy. He answered my prayer."

"But," said Tobias, "The entrails -"

"Are merely entrails. They hold no power over man, demon, or Angel of God." The Angel blinked its thousand eyes, and Tobias felt something wriggling inside him, swimming up his windpipe. Choking, gagging, reaching desperately for his throat, he keeled over, and fell to the floor, dead.

A fish popped out of his mouth, flopping uselessly on the floor. Kneeling down, Sarah shut his staring eyes, closed his open mouth, and whispered gently.

"Be not afraid."

Andrew Davis

The Seventh Time They Fucked For The Last Time (Or The Slow Painful Death of a Toxic Affair)

Beam of sunlight
Between almost closed curtains
Blue hued cigarette smoke swirls
Dancing in caresses of air
Furiously losing themselves in each other

Reforming like despair
Looking for a plight
To feed on
Or a soul to haunt
Something to ruin
With the spell of spite
It needs to cast
To sustain itself

Before the breeze intrudes
And the smoke clears
Or the sun moves on
From shining on
The inertia of
Fucking for the
Last time again

Slowly fade the echoes
Of memory recall

They were a blank page
An unopened book
A dream undreamed

Time not yet tasted

All seeming possible
In the blink of light
Piercing the fugue
Of lonely nothingness

The one star saving the sky
From complete emptiness
The magical, the precious

The coming, the going
The always promising
The what may become
Of right now
The realisation
The resignation to drifting
The bodies still meeting
The inevitable ending
This time
Maybe

William Dean Ford

Fingers and Toes

Precious newborn, little fingers and toes,
wrapping around my finger, soft and unflinching.
Grabbing my thumb, connecting,
this child of mine, gentle and full of life

Hours spent, holding him in my arms,
until my muscles ache, but I don't let him go.
Sleeping, warm, soft, so new, this future begun,
my precious newborn, little fingers and toes

Warm skin turns cold, and I want to hold him,
keeping him warm, nestled in my arms.
But I can't, I can only watch,
frozen in the distance as the doctors work

And I watch him now, with those little fingers and toes,
sleeping beneath the web of wires and pads.
The constant beep of monitors, and the holding of breath,
And I wait,

and watch,
and wait,
and watch,
and wait

They said it was common, he was in the right place,
they gave him a syndrome and all the right care.
But all I can do is hold my breath and count the beeps,
And watch the numbers go up,

and down

How much is too much? How much is too low?
I've seen the doctors resuscitate my son,
and I'm waiting for the beeps and the numbers,
holding my breath for the next panic to come

And he sleeps.

Small and fragile under his nest of wires
Unaware of the pain,
and the panic and fear,
that comes with the beep,

Beep
Beep
Beep
Beep

I can't hold him, but I can give him my thumb,
his tiny, fragile fingers wrapping firm.
Connecting, life, that bond between us,
in his fragile slumber on the little glass bed

Eleven days.
Of waiting, of trying to live.
And we know the medication, we know the signs,
and with terror and hope, we can take him home

And I can hold him in my arms again,
Heavy and soft and warm until my muscles ache.

But I'm not letting him go again
My precious child, little fingers and toes

Baz Greenland

Blood and balls.

There is a tale to the scar over my eye,
it begins down the Gower, 'neath cloudless sky.
A tale of two families, stumps, bat, bails and ball,
"We're in need of a backstop!" goes out the call.
So up steps I, with fist on chest, and
with a confident voice says "I'll do my best.".
It was not just I who'd raised my hand,
someone was standing where the backstop should stand.
Unwilling to lose what had been mine to win,
I decided to stand a bit closer than him.

The ball left bowlers hand and flew towards I,
the batsman swung, crack! and blood filled my eye.
Time froze in the campsite as the sound echoed round.
All eyes fell on me, as I screamed on the ground.
As grown ups ran up, you could hear them all think,
"I can't take him to hospital, we've all had a drink."
So 'neath the cloudless, cornflower sky,
two half pissed nurses taped up my eye.

Andy Caruana

Bad Sport

He said he'd never met a boy
who didn't like football.
He said in all his years
he'd never met a boy who didn't
like football.
On the pitch, between the posts,
tripping over two left clichés,
aim awry, tangled ankles,
tripping over nothing
that was always in his way.

He sloped off the sports field,
found a corner to curl in,
caved in to the craving
for silence and solace.
It was simple, really.
He was just a boy
who didn't like football.
But with a brain full of books,
he got his kicks elsewhere.

Bryan Marshall

Joe

'Do you know my brother?' asks the big-eyed child
with a flop of butterscotch hair
and the ghost of chickenpox darning his cheeks.

'I do not know your brother? I tell the wide-eyed child
with the grass-stained shirt and joyfully scuffed trainers
that flash like paparazzi when he runs.

'You don't know Joe?' cries the saucer-eyed child,
aghast, as though I am unfamiliar with the king,
chocolate-daubed chin dropping open.

'He's in Miss Bevan's class,' says the round-eyed child
with three missing teeth and one loose
that he likes to tease with his tongue.

'I have not met Joe,' I say with regret as the huge-eyed child
regales me with tales of heroism and chivalry:
fishing a distressed football down from a tree,
coming nearly-second on sports day,
sharing chocolate when he wasn't even made to,
giving hugs when you fell into nettles and it hurt very much.

With a scab on his elbow and a hole in his jumper
the large-eyed child shakes his head in wonderment
that there are people in the world
who don't know Joe.

Rachel Badger

& then you came along

for the past week, i felt like a mist, gathering –
pouring myself into shoes & buses & office meeting rooms with
a mind dis   per   sing like gas. & my focus rolling out like
                                clouds roll across the
                      mountain.

it's a tuesday & i've spent the whole day trying to
fun   –nel myself into a solid.
trying to touch computer keys & house keys.
buying milk from a shop just to feel
                      present to the cashier for a moment.
but i fumble the eye contact, & drift away,
                    feeling imprecise & incorporeal.

all of what ails me is so nameless & complicated:
a hundred separate things, or nothing at all.
a bad day, or a bad gut, or a string of bad relationships.
i am
                                        lost to it

until, on a bus, i arrive to you
inconsolable to the toy you dropped from your highchair.
i retrieve it & return it to your hand

and your red face
dramatically inhales
and breaks out in a smile.

i mop your
tiny face of tiny tears
and you giggle.

problems so solvable, so tangible.
you smile and i see you've grown
another stumpy tooth so you now have four peeking through.
incomplete but full of promises.

you still can't speak - but you say one word - "hiya!"
loudly and constantly, it is still new and novel enough for me to break
into smiles of my own and say back, constantly, "hiya"

you've learned to point, and everything is pointed at,
                                      "this!" you point,

        "*that*!" you point,
and the adults around you comply with their tiny queen.
calm and direct, you are the eye of a personal hurricane.

everyone folds to you and your order, happily:
your grandparents, your parents,

                                        even my gathering mist.

Dervla O'Brien

Gnawing

i have a family of mice living inside my bed. we have a divan.
i just want to know what they're doing all the time
because of the novelty, because i am not a mouse
but whenever i open the underbed draw, they run about
in a tizzy
and stop doing their mouse things

they don't let me see what they're up to
they scurry off, little secret keepers,
hide in corners as i trace
inscrutable cave scratchings
with fingers

i want to write to them
please let me see what you're doing
when you're doing what you do when
i'm not watching
because i have a curiosity, because
                only that's as far as i get

there's no way for me to force them
to give up the inner details of their lives
so i lie in the dark and listen
sussing out what their nights entail
eyes wet and peeled like clams worn down
by the sea

Alexander Winter

When I Say Rhythm

Every day is the
same. Having
trouble shutting
down, shutting up, lying

flat in the tinted
triangle of the revolving door,
feet sticking stiffly out
as person after person
slams and pushes until something –

    Transmitters. Signal in, signal out.
Sine wave, square wave,
pain. Fresh produce, Sackler's Farm.
Press the button. Press it again.

I'm at my crystal ball, wreathed
in mist. The glass clears,
but I turn away - *adverts*. Someone with no
mouth to feed. I can't steal crumbs.

In the middle lane it's dark, two
trucks on each side. But
there's a downhill coming,
    maybe light.

Gordon Anderson

3 minutes.

3 minutes tonight is
a subconscious argument whether
to wait here or go to the pub, which goes
a lot longer than you'd think.
It's 16 3-minute songs
of angry punk and an 18minute
live EP with orchestral accompaniment
and xylophones.
It's more rain than has
ever fallen from the sky in 3
minutes. It's a time loop of watching
a 3 (possibly older but I'm stuck
on 3 now) year old running far too
close to moving traffic, while the
father talks on his phone then steals
her shoe and points out the glass
on the floor that reflects
the crimson shine of pixels that
are promising the 9 is still
due on time.
In 3 minutes.

Andy Caruana

Fluid. Singular.

I blow somebody's cigarette smoke from the path of another person's cigarette smoke.

"They're so graceful, aren't they?" another person asks no-one in-particular as they glide into the room, nodding at the ice-skaters on the television.

They plonk down a big bowl of maize-based snacks. Think of them as like Monster Munch, but cheap and probably salt and vinegar flavoured.

The ice-skating duo salchow beyond one another before doubling back into a sequinned embrace. Fluid. Singular.

"So, I don't think my new personal trainer likes me," somebody on the adjacent sofa says before taking a swig from their pint glass filled with Baileys.

"No?" the person sitting next to them asks.

"They keep trying to make me do pull ups."

"...yeah, cool. Hey, could you pass me those?"

I hold out the bowl for their short fluid-inflated fingers to grasp.

"You're not even listening!"

"I am! I am! They want you to do push ups."

"Pull ups!"

"Yeah, whatever!" Crumbs cascade down their shirt.

Someone's cigarette smoke loops around another person's cigarette smoke. An embrace. Fluid. Singular.

Simon Read

Care

An almost-complete china set,
plates delicate as my skull,
glitters in the washing-up bowl.
I wipe each piece with gentle strokes
and leave each one to dry
in the sun that tries to burn its way
through the soft-pulse, limpid cold.

I wait till they shine,
bright as winter daybreak,
then place them with care
into a cupboard bright with glass.

I close the door, stand and stare
at this almost-complete china set,
knowing that one day
more pieces will be
lost, bro-
ken.

Bryan Marshall

Reclining Chair

It's her safety.
Her resting laurels.
Her crutch.

A bed,
or spectator's perch.
A halfway house

between immobility
and the nursing home.
It tips her up
to quiver and shake
the gauntlet to
the be-railed porcelain.

It's her haven,
her trap.
A reminder of vulnerability.
Life can't have become this claustrophobic triangle
of chair, kettle, commode.
Or can it? She wonders.

Oh how she wishes,
the chair could assist
her everywhere.

Through this world
not built for the meek.
For her aged body.

Spent and crumbled
bent and humbled.
By time.Even the chair
can't protect her from that.
Everything recedes.

Atrophic brain,
entropic mind.
Managed ergonomic decline.

But some things
won't be taken-
at least not in reclining gradations.

She'll remember joy, love and faith
as almost everything recedes.
Almost everything.

Osian Luke

Adrenochrome

Adrenochrome, Adrenochrome, Adrenochrome
What happens to children stolen from their home?
Adrenochrome, Adrenochrome, Adrenochrome
The antithesis to God's recommended home.

Love is not a cortisol. Truth.

Francess

The Angel Hotel

He sits at the front,
mouthing at the whiteboard,
chewing
on foreign sound,
concentration needle-fine.

His words fall
wrong
on the paper,
alphabet twisted,
cricking its neck
consonants spasming on the page.

We coax pictures
from his hands
with our plastic-bright smiles.
He offers a house,
a family,
a dog,
its tongue snaking
red and wet between oversized teeth.

We do not ask about the dog,
the family,
the house.
His life now is condensed
Arial font, size 10
A few lines of email:
A name, a date of birth, a city crumpled in on itself.

There are oceans between each line.
Dust-particled oxygen feathering lungs,
Mewling harmonising sirens,
Fifty-year old plates, fractured, wedding gifts too heavy
to carry.

His current address is a room on the fifth floor
Relatives huddled behind a do-not-disturb sign.
Some of them.

Rachel Badger

The Recording Angel

I speak the names of the dead.

Every winter's eve, I heave my soul from root to branch, to shape my speech around the name of one who yet lives. Within a year, without exception, prayer or reprieve, they die.
I am the speaker not the spindle; that thread of fate which drags the names of the damned from me, is woven by hands other than mine.

Do not judge me. You cannot know.

If there is a being older than I, I know them not. This land is part of me and I a part of it, but we are not the same. One side lies a border, the other a sea; my roots broach them both. I have seen each rise and fall and change and rise anew. I did not speak, then, in that time before names.

Until they gave one to me.

They call me a spirit. *Angelystor.* Evangelist, Angel, Chronicler. Of those the last I suit best. I am a tale of many, my skin a skein of history. Time twists itself in rings through me, a living record not quite alive, but which can never die. I cannot have that which I must give: the snap of the cord at the first and last moments of life. But neither can I leaven a thing with life, only with the knowing of its death. I am a warden, a warning, a murderer –

No, not that. *Never* that. They die, but not by my hand. Can you be thought a killer if your only crime is to divine?

Yet I am condemned to watch. They crawl to me for mercy on bleeding palms. I learned that word from those who showed none but spoke of it as if they did. But whether they fall upon blades or into the sea's brackish throat, none escape my voice.

I do not bite, but I do devour. Where they fall, bone and flesh and muscle grow themselves into the ground, into me. I pull them down into the gullet of the earth until they lie so far below me I can drink them like rain.

To do otherwise would be a waste.

Memory is pain until spoken. I was seared in two before memory began. I do not remember how. It could be that the sky's blazing dagger cut me into fragments. Perhaps I was formed like this, as of two great arms shooting up from the earth, frozen in ascension.

Between two trunks lies a yawning gulf where a heart should be. One bears a twisting cluster of bark, a swirl of wound wood. It may look like a human heart, yet it does not beat like one. It beats to the drumming of feet, the hammering of nails; the thick, viscous gush of tearing muscle. It beats to the echo of conquest, when invaders made us strangers in our own land. Cymru, *countrymen, friends*, became Wales, *foreigners, outsiders*. They had not the axes to cut me down, nor the strength to move me as they moved the standing stones of our land to a foreign plain.

My heart may be gone but the rest remains.

I do not need one. What good could it do me, something soft and fleshy to pierce? Even now, they cannot hear me scream. But I do hear them. Buds sprout from their tears, lichen from their ichor. I cannot weave the warp and the weft of their lives, only mark where the thread will snap.

Only one has yet to doubt me. His name sings through me even now. Ale made him bold, brought him to me clumsy and pawing in the drenched dark. He came to make me a myth. I made him memory.

He deserved it. As a boy, I had sheltered him from the rain. There are none to shelter me.

Save for one.

A Prince of Cernyw came to my land and knelt before me. His eyes were made of sky and they wept like oceans, and from his sweet mouth issued prayers in his mother tongue and mine. It moved me, that he knew my language, the language of valley and mountain, a language older than stone, birthed so long ago I watched it amass. He christened me holy and built me a sacred place of my own.

Llangernyw.

He wandered often in my land, once it bore his name. He would walk under my canopy; run soft, unbattled hands over me and feed me his prayers.

I was his truest altar. And yet his name I spoke when his time was done.

If I could weep, I would have then. He did not. Neither did he rage when he heard his own name as a portent. He could have burned my limbs from under me, starved my earthen bed, turned me to ash and smoke like so many of his kind had tried. Had I mouth to speak all save doom, I would have bade him carve me into deadwood to warm his brittle bones; to let me curl around him like a flaming cage.

They built him a tomb, but he does not rest there. He lies with me, in the place where a heart should be. He used to look up at me with his eyes of sky and weep at my beauty. Now they have mouldered in their sockets, I look up and find his gaze in the sky, and the rain is as the cooling balm of his tears.

I see you. The summer breeze tugs at your hair as you near me. Your cool hands stroke my coarse bark, gentleness as I have not felt in such an aching long time. I feel the blood coursing through your flesh, alive and hot and throbbing and so unlike the old, cold gore congealed in my roots. Your eyes are made of sky.

I speak your name.

Barbara Hughes-Moore

A Lovely Verse

Say it
But say it beautifully

Those worms eating up your guts,
And those thick gouges in your skull,
Tell us all about them
But in a way that makes us nod our heads,
Catch our breaths, and say;
"Wow, that's beautiful."

Don't say any dumb shit like
"I wanna fucking kill myself."
Or
"I'm gonna slit my fucking wrists."

Tell us, instead, with a lovely metaphor
About some overripe cherries
Falling from their stalks
When the farmer forgets to pick them.

Say it beautifully,
Make it worth our while.
Or don't say anything at all.

Alexander Winter

Crown Of Creation

Out of sight, forgotten in my stony tomb
The roar of wave and winter storm
Closer by each passing year
Till all around me slips and crashes
And I fall again
To a new place of rest
Undercliff

And now you appear and raise me to your face

Your eyes I see marvel
At the still-perfect imprint of my spiral shell
Insensate though to you I seem, imagine
I embody all that the Earth has learnt
More sentient and alert than you
In your too slow growth toward
Planetary consciousness

In talk with your fellow fossil-hunters
I hear the boast that eras after I was buried
Your species has gained pre-eminence
During Earth's latest blink of geological time
To become the crown of its creation

And from your mouth the words Lyme Regis
Set me wondering if in this king's town you conceive
How you may be dethroned
Your crown to fall like me to the bottom of a muddy sea
Or melt in overheated atmosphere
If not already evaporated

By global thermonuclear war
While from my ammonite graveyard
On Monmouth Beach
I am left where you dropped me
To observe your future
My fossil eyes
Watching just another twist
And turn in Life's cycle of evolution
And extinction

Pete Gaskell

Salvation

> Revelation 21

The End is the beginning of the word endorphin
The End is the beginning of The Word
The End is the beginning of Love's promise
To end Manmade trauma, grief and pain.

To end inner turmoil and confusion
To end abuse, regret and shame
To end the sickness of mind delusion
To end the trauma, grief and pain.

The End is the beginning of The Word endorphin
The End is the beginning of The Word
The End is the beginning of God's promise
To end Manmade trauma, grief and pain.

The End is the promise of Salvation
The End is the promise of re birth
The end is the conscious healing message
For Peace and Heaven here on Earth.

The End is the beginning of the word endorphin
The End is the beginning of The Word
The End is the beginning of Love's promise
To end Manmade trauma, grief and pain.

The End is the promise of New Heaven
Where truth will set us free from pain
Where mourning will be completed
For Love to reside in us again.

The End is the beginning of The Word endorphin
Where 'the stones will cry out' for rebirth
The end is the beginning of The Word endorphin
For Peace and Heaven here on Earth.

Francess

sound of a break

A few nights ago I dreamt again
about the pen knife, pressing against
harp strings. Twanging back, the pieces
like weapons; retaliating violence to the blade.

At your house, years ago, I was noseying
in your top cupboard, and down rained the contents.

A wine glass, smashed and tinkling like wind chimes,
even worse, a green marble pestle and mortar.
An antique from your recently dead great uncle.
A chunk smashed out, flown —

At work, they say I'm too timid of breaking things,
say I should just try my best, problem solve the rest. But
computers are the only part of life which brag a reset button.

On the days I have to spare, I bury myself in the work of
building things.
I study the construction of a sentence, a table, a bridge,
a government.

I try and build a story, a home, a community, a self.
I pour hours of myself like cement to fill the gaps
between us.

Try and build a liferaft from our laughter in the middle
of the night.
I feel like a Roman when I see what I have managed.
Half-excavation. Half-stone carved pillars.
I am holding with all my strength,

until the rain pours in.

Hadn't you agreed? Hadn't you agreed to make a roof?
Shingles or thatched or tin-pan sheets — I didn't care,
I'd understood.
The rain poured in, the cement not yet set, the wooden frame
splintering,

sounding exactly like a lurch inside a stomach.
We've been speaking, and it's like trying to put my hands
in my pockets,

but hearing eggshells cracking —
clear, cold, goop, slopping against my probing fingers.

Dervla O'Brien

Mother of the Sad Clowns

She gave me her pizazz, her playful accents-
love of music and tongue for a good story

An orator's flourish she inherited from a middling man whose
confidence doesn't care if you don't get the joke:
you're going to laugh anyway.

Confidence suspended over a chasm

A jolly hostess persona- hyperactive charm—
highbrow aspirations with a school teacher's patience
that doesn't shatter but *snaps*
Sizzling, Simmering anger- rising tin pot top.

I have your tendency to fear the worst
and not rejoice for the best.
A methodist's work ethic; a method I could never regiment.

Chattering anxieties and Hyper-looped earworms writhe Over
one
another
Intrusive choruses of inspiration, Monsoons of ideas
Drought after the deluge, Performing happiness, Day after
dreary day.

We have these tortures in common.
The never-ending dialogue of
confetti-
falling

ideas
.

So I submit to citalopram,
distrust my own stuttering heart.
You gave me these gifts

Gifts I only noticed
once I entered the self-therapeutic mode where
every event was skinned,
dissected on the chopping board.
I want to give them back— these tainted, bloody alloys—
but I can't give back the tails and not the heads.

So I keep on performing
and hear from my lips your jolly charm of a smile
knowing that all the while
you've been sobbing just like me.

Osian Luke

Letter to my family

Relatively speaking, I no longer have a family.
Instead, I have a battalion of crazed wild boar seeking to impale.

I have flags, torn, half masted, struggling to flutter,
while around me, archers pin me to the spot.

Searching for the familiar, I have discovered my people.
Not those who would tie me, flog me, leave me stunted,

tied to a post of family ties and blood and water and
I don't know where I am going with this.

The battle metaphor ran away with the horses that
pull the carriage containing your body. Familial

similes trip on my tongue. I am tired. But I have
yet to serve sentry so I stay awake, in lieu of the wake

I am denied entry to. That was a bit trite wasn't it?
Next I shall be writing imagery of the night, the long dark night,

but go gently dad. Put down your burden. Go to the big dominos game in the sky.
Ignore the cries of too soon, too soon, for though we hadn't quite finished

the conversation we were having, know I heard you when your last ever word was in defence of me. Know that those who count are sharing their memories with me.

They're sharing tales of the things you told them, but never said to me.
I wish you had said them to me.
I would have been ok if you had said them to me.
But hearing it through their mouths. Words like, love, proud of

treasured, apple, eye. It is easier to believe that no matter how long
how much time, from so far away, across oceans from the island

I inherited as a birthmark, that my birthright was to be loved
in a way that could not have helped me. Even towards the end

you barely got to know me and now your other children
guard your corpse jealously. Have been plain in their disdain

for the sister who just wanted to see if we could make peace,
however uneasily. Not to be. Not to be.

They tell me you fought till the end, as if there could ever be an end
to the man, the myth, the legend. Man like Lloyd.

Dee Dickens

Our Mother Tongue

No, not that one.
Not the sticky strings of phonemes
we extract from our larynx,
notes that we use to shape the air;
when we were small and excitable things,
squeals and chortles
rattled out of us,
our mouths wide and vulnerable.
We didn't need to be witty or quick or wry.
We laughed like frogs kicking through water,
easy and unconscious,
giggles dribbling through the spaces in our fingers
as we spun and spun and spun until we were sick.
But adolescence ironed out our feral edges.
We studied hard how to be cool,
how to be normal,
colouring within the lines we gave ourselves,
rebelling in perfect harmony.
And we lost, along with our baby teeth,
that knack of laughing
as though we were fluent.

Rachel Badger

The Internal Friction of Those Required To Bow

Soapy sponge squeak against crockery
Remnants of regret soak in the suds
Unwisely taken actions glimmer in rainbow grease
Taking the sunlight and eviscerating it
On the surface of the water

Claustrophobia of bubbles bursting
Sharp blades lay traps out of sight
Not yet learned the trick of
Leave the knives out, do them last
Lessons delivered in slices
Of red running pain

Sharks of sharp self talk
Circle the wound
Air bluer than when
Big toe meets bed leg
Plaster bluer than any food
So it won't be served to diners
If it falls off

Catering to the wishes of all but oneself
Cleaning up after the feeding of all but oneself
Eating after everyone else
All work to the assistants
All compliments to The Chef

William Dean Ford

For They/Them

i showed up today
for myself
for my safety
to push back
against all they
minimise
while maxing out my credit
pushing boundaries
violating parameters
ley lines abused
barriers burned
bullying gets blurred
county line corruption

some of us break free
most get reminded of place
we all get asked to contribute
sat at a temporary table
offered a decaying seat
and for a micro-moment i think i can speak

i believe the manifesto
of equality, ethics, equity, elevation
my heart pounds me to speak up
even though my voice shakes
cos that's what mami taught me to do
until they cut out her tongue
stuffed her throat with glass marbles
and i gaslight myself that i can do better

that i can belong

and those with the hammer
sat around this quaint-kitsch-hipster-shit say "shh shh shh"
and one by one the marginalised leave
without fight
the fury fills their lungs
until there is no more breath left to even panic

Rufus Mufasa

Pony and Birds – Stephen Andrews

with special thanks to People Speak Up

Biographies

Alexander Winter is an English-born writer currently living in Taffs Well having found his way there through a Creative Writing BA at Aberystwyth and subsequently a Creative Writing MA at Cardiff University. He has previously been published in Roath Writers' *To The Sofa and Back Again* (2020, 2021), *Cardiff Writing Circle's 75th Anniversary Anthology* (2022), *CWMA's Sing and Eventually Weep Tonight* (2023) and *RCT's Creative Writing Anthology* (2023). Aside from writing, he has a wife, three cats and far too many hobbies.

"**Andy [Caruana]** must be one of the laziest people in the world." –Direct quote from GCSE geography teacher. School report. 1991.

Andrew Davis is a writer based in Cardiff. His prose and poetry has been published in anthologies and online journals by independent publishers including Abergavenny Small Press, Fictive Dream and Bending Genres.

Barbara Hughes-Moore is a scholar and lecturer of law and literature, based in Cardiff University. She specialises in criminal law, Gothic fiction, and the rhetorical and cultural intersections between literary and legal works, and she is currently working on a book that illuminates how 'monsters' in Gothic fiction can reveal the 'monstrousness' of the criminal law from the nineteenth century to now. Her fiction, too, is very much in the Gothic mould, concerned as it is with spectres, ghouls and hauntings – psychological or otherwise. Her short stories have been published by *Horror Scribes*

('Wednesday's Child' won their Fright Cards competition in 2016) and *The Folks* literary magazine. She blogs about her work and her writing on: https://thelawlass.wordpress.com/

Baz Greenland began working on his first novel when he was 10. He finally achieved his goal of being published at 38. Baz hadn't looked at a poem since finishing his A-Level English Literature at 19 but found a new appreciation for reading and writing poetry, when he joined Roath Writers this year.
Joining Roath Writers and finding a writing community to express his passion with, has been one of highlights of this year. Baz has discovered that poetry is a wonderful vehicle for exploring his past. All the poems he has written processed something about his terrible childhood, or his own love for his children in defiance of that past. It has been a gift to share them with such a welcoming and talented community!

Bryan Marshall plays with words in a host of various ways, putting down symbols willy-nilly just as thoughts occur to him, arbitrarily jotting down scrawlings of fluctuating quality that occasionally pop into his mind, outlandish and curious as it is.
This biography was partially brought to you through a conscious option on his part not to, until now, use the letter 'e'.

Dee Dickens is a writer. Some days she is trying to make the world feel things in an attempt to make people nicer to each other. On other days, she is just trying.

Dervla O'Brien is a writer and software engineer from South Armagh. She writes about the intersecting and contradictory worlds she grew up in: traditional rural Ireland, by the border between the North and South in the aftermath of the peace process; and much more scaring, the comments sections of early

YouTube videos. She also writes an ungodly number of love poems for trees. She is a member of the Belfast-based SoupInk. Collective and Crescent Arts Writers, as well as the Cardiff-based Roath Writers Group. This year, she joined Belfast Community circus. She can't fully unicycle or juggle yet, but has all the makings of a wonderful clown.

Francess, with her 40 years of studying and working with the healing arts as a Holistic Health and Beauty Therapist, identifies emotional links between mind, body and spirit. Francess explores boundaries of Love and fear emotionally, physiologically, environmentally and psychologically in search of health, happiness and healing. After the Kinesiology technique of muscle testing was challenged as a form of divination by some Christians, Francess studied scripture for the healing message of Christ and conveys her understandings in her words with appreciation for the miracle of life and Oneness through Love for all. From the stars to the star fish her work addresses all in between to inspire Peace, Love and Joy for healing and kindness to All Nations for Peace and Heaven on Earth. Frances changed her name to Francess to affirm the feminine.

Francess has numerous publications in poetry magazines, Chapter 9 Time for Heaven on Earth in best seller Inspirational Women in Business, IWOW. She has self-published 3 books available on Amazon: *Healing Poems for Positive Love, Parousia Love's Light, Parousia Book of Life* and 3 CD's: *Ultimate Healing Poems, Parousia Love's Light, Parousia Armageddon.* Also Parousia Scroll of Life, New Jerusalem Heavenly Scrolls used for protest against all abuse and injustice to end grief, suffering, hurt and pain for justice and peace. www.Francess.org

Gordon Anderson is a Cardiff-based writer of poems and flash fiction, now also working on creative essays. Part of the Literature Wales '(Re)Writing Wales' cohort of 2023, he has adjusted to life as a serious writer by buying a nice pair of corduroys. His poems have been published in *Break-Up Hex, Horses Are Just Big Dogs* and, due to a typing error, *The Pottery Review*.

Mat Troy is a Cardiff based writer and performer. Some of his favorite projects to date have included co-writing the screenplay for Agents of LOVCRAFT, which reached the finals of the UK Sitcom trials; Dust and Dandruff, a bioplay of the poets Ivor Cutler and Phyllis King; and his first poem in Welsh which was included the 125 Objects exhibition at the Dinefwr National Trust estate. Mat has been published in, among others, *The Ghastling Magazine, Neon Literary, Just Snails surreal fiction zine, the ASP journal* and the *Carrion Press*. Mat is a sketch writer for *Welcome Strangers* sketch show on BBC Radio Wales. His current project, the audio drama, *Somnambulance Driver*, is currently in pre-production.

Osian Luke is a Cardiff-based writer who writes predominantly in English. He would describe himself as a silver-tongued doom-monger who, very occasionally, can produce a passable piece of humour or optimism. His work centers on themes of hope and despair; more specifically on love and loss, climate change and the future, mental health and illness, as well as politics and philosophy. Yeats' 'The Second Coming' is a continual source of inspiration and existential dread for Osian. In terms of writing aspirations, he has written novels which he hopes will one day be published and intends to publish at least one collection of poetry. For Osian, the process of writing poetry is meditation, therapy, prophecy, and thought-experimentation all-in-one. "I love poetry as a craft; it offers an ephemeral retreat from our experience into the curated moments of others. Poetry is indelibly subjective, and I'm always amazed by the sheer variety of wondrous words that poets come up with. It's truly an art for everyone, and that's why I love it; whether that's reading, listening, watching, or writing it myself."

Pete Gaskell, conscious of the risk he runs of being Jack of all trades but master on none, writes fiction, reviews, poetry and plays. He has had poems published in *Poetica*, the *Atlanta Review, Places of Poetry* and *Love The Words Anthology* for Dylan Day 2021& 2022 (discoverdylanthomas.com). Pete reviews theatre, books, film, and concerts for *Wales Arts Review* and *Get The Chance*. In July 2022, he won the 75 word flash fiction competition run by Cardiff Writers' Circle as well as performance pieces for a walking tour of Cardiff, part of their 75th Anniversary celebrations.

After gaining a Masters degree from University of South Wales in Scriptwriting, Pete's screenplay 'Pigs in Muck' featured in the Lockdown Monologue Film Festival 2020, and his drama about Lloyd George was performed in theatres across South Wales.
It's his draft novel *Shaman's Blues* he most desires to publish though, and is looking forward to learning some of the tools of the trade at Roath Writers publishing party.

Rachel Badger enjoys writing, tea, reading and other cat-lady pursuits. She would probably get more things published if the words agreed to sit still on the page.

Rufus Mufasa is a pioneering participatory artist who advocates hip hop education and poetry development accessible to all. Lyricist, rapper and performance art poet, with an MA in scriptwriting. Rufus is a Hay Writer at Work, supports several intergenerational projects, mentors men at Parc Prison and is planning her fourth visit to Finland, where she recently headlined the Helsinki Literature Festival. As well as being the first Welsh artist to perform at Ruisrock festival, she mentors Finnish beat poets, and now writes trilingually as a result.

Simon Read has been a member of Roath Writers since day one, contributing words and covers for the anthologies. He has an extensive publishing history, spanning novellas, poetry chapbooks, short story collections, comics, and graphic novellas. Currently in the final stages of his Creative Writing PhD, Simon also holds MA and BA English & Creative Writing qualifications from Cardiff Metropolitan University, where he also teaches. Simon enjoys the works of Richard Brautigan, Kurt Vonnegut, and Tom Robbins who, by complete coincidence, write in a similar style to him. Simon's favourite comment received about his creative writing is "You often omit what would usually be considered information critical to driving a story, instead opting to exaggerate the minutiae... which is fascinatingly disorientating and somehow works."

William Dean Ford is an adaptable creative writer who performs spoken word material. He recently became the host of a Wellness themed Radio Cardiff Show playing upbeat music and reading out relevant poetry, including his own bespoke material created for the weekly show, exploring aspects of Voice. Eclectic in nature, William's material may be read, recited, rapped or even sung by him, whichever form of delivery best suits the form of the material. The literal and authorial voice of the material is similarly adapted to best suit the subject and intended audience.

When not writing, you may find William photographing random things around Cardiff. He has sold several prints and exhibited some. One of his pictures can be found as the cover image of a poetry collection by Topher Mills (*Sex on Toast*, Parthian Books). Early into the 2020 Lockdown, William was commissioned by the local health board to write seventeen weekly 'Poetry Prescriptions' responding to the developing situation. These pieces reflected some of the range of William's approaches to writing, literal, figurative, satirical, heartfelt, imaginative, surreal, playful, cynical and blunt. He aims to surprise himself with what he writes, to be consistent in application but diverse in results.

Printed in Great Britain
by Amazon